A WORLD OF ANIMALS

by DANA CARROLL

With the Editors of TIME For Kids

Mc Graw Hill Macmillan McGraw-Hill

Dolphins have **fins** to swim.

Polar bears have thick fur
to keep warm.

Elephants have **trunks** to pick up food.

Beavers have long teeth
to cut tree branches.

Woodpeckers have sharp beaks to peck wood.

Camels have big **hooves**
to walk on sand.

Glossary

 fin (FIN) the body part that helps fish, whales, or dolphins swim *(page 2)*

 hooves (HOOVZ) the hard feet of camels and some other animals *(page 7)* Plural of **hoof** (HOOF)

 trunk (TRUNGK) the snout of an elephant *(page 4)*

Index